So You're

60!

summersdale

SO YOU'RE 60!

Illustrations by Andy Hammond

Summersdale Publishers Ltd
46 West Street
Chichester
West Sussex
PO19 1RP
UK

www.summersdale.com

Printed and bound by Tien Wah Press, Singapore

ISBN: 1-84024-564-6
ISBN 13: 978-1-84024-564-6

So You're

60!

A Handbook for the Newly Confused

Mike Haskins & Clive Whichelow

INTRODUCTION

Well look at you!

Congratulations! You are 60 years young!

I said CONGRATULATIONS, DEAR! YOU'RE 60 YEARS YOUNG! YES!

Idiots who talk to you like that are going to irritate the hell out of you from now on.

Yes, you're 60. But so what?

60's not old these days is it? You don't feel old, do you? You don't look old.

OK, you don't look *that* old.

You're the same as ever. Nothing's changed. Nothing's improved that much but nothing's changed either. You're fit as a flea.

A flea whose knees are giving him a bit of gyp maybe. But still basically fit.

OK, there's that pain in your neck as well. And that funny thing you can feel round the back somewhere which you really must try to look at in the mirror some time.

But apart from that there's nothing much wrong. It's not as though you've gone gaga.

So what if you can't immediately remember your children's names? What's wrong with having to run through the names of all of them in sequence till you hit the right answer?

60 is a great age to be – in more ways than one! Particularly when you've got this handy little volume to take the rise out of all the idiotic preconceptions people have about old codgers like you.

I beg your pardon.

People in their prime like you.

So let me just say in conclusion, I think you're marvellous for your age. I said I THINK YOU'RE MARVELLOUS FOR YOUR AGE, DEAR! YES!

Here's to the next 60 years!

THE BASIC MYTHS ABOUT TURNING 60

You'll be able to enjoy a nice, long, well-earned
rest – and that's just after
walking up the stairs.

You're a sort of elder statesperson to the rest of the family – this means you were voted out of office years ago and everything you say now is regarded as a potential embarrassment to the current administration.

You'll spend the rest of your days on long luxurious cruises – if you regard visits to the local clinic and chemist as a cruise, that is.

You'll be treated with respect everywhere you go – as long as you only go places where you'll meet other people the same age as you.

You brought up and looked after your children all these years, now it's their time to look after you – unless they decide to sub-contract the job to the local branch of rough-looking Care Workers R Us.

THINGS YOU WILL
NEVER NOW DO

 Fancy someone older than yourself

 Break any of your bad habits

 Learn to ski

 Be the new face of Estée Lauder

Get the hang of computers

YOUR *LIFE* WILL NOW CONSIST OF

 Sleeping during sex instead of after it

 Going to more funerals than weddings

 Being told to slow down by your GP rather than by the police

 Having the *Radio Times* as your social calendar for the week

DRESS CODE FOR THE OVER 60s – SOME DO'S & DON'TS

Don't take fashion advice from anyone older than yourself.

Do remember – almost anything
goes with grey.

Don't buy sturdy clothes because they'll
'see you out'.

Do wear the psychedelic dayglo fashions of
your youth – not only will people see you
coming, it'll be easier for you to find your
clothes in the dark.

Don't try wearing a thong – your flesh may resemble a bunch of uncooked sausages stuffed in a string bag.

Don't wear anything *skin tight* – especially as these days your skin might not be *skin tight* either.

Don't try out young people's fashions; they aren't going to suit you – you'll just have to dress tastefully instead.

17

CULTURE CONVERTER

When speaking with people younger than
yourself it's no use talking about things that
happened before they were born; they won't
have a clue what you're on about. So here is
a handy culture converter to translate your
cultural reference points to their equivalent:

Culture Converter

Category	60+	Middle-aged	Early middle-aged	Young People
Early memory	End of rationing	The harsh winter of '62	Dad being on strike	Sing along to Kylie
Pop shock	Elvis joining the army	The Beatles splitting up	Bowie 'quitting'	Robbie leaving Take That
Parent alienating comedy	*The Goon Show*	*Monty Python*	*The Young Ones*	*Little Britain*
Fab radio	Luxemburg	Radio Caroline	Radio 1	Something cool off the internet
Catchphrase	'He's fallen in the water'	'Nudge nudge, wink wink'	'Fascist!'	'I'm a lady!'
Childhood food	Whale meat	Tinned fruit	Instant mash	Pizza
Childhood clothes	Double-breasted raincoat	Duffle coat	Bomber jacket	Anything with the right brand name

WELL-KNOWN PEOPLE CURRENTLY IN THEIR 60s

When you think about it, being 60 is THE generation to belong to. For starters it's the generation that all of The Beatles, The Kinks, The Who, Diana Ross and The Supremes, Bob Dylan, The Byrds, The Velvet Underground, Smokey Robinson, Pink Floyd, David Bowie and The Rolling Stones belong to.

I know that's come as an enormous shock to you but it's true – The Rolling Stones are still only in their 60s. Here's a small selection of other well-known people now in their 60s:

Joanna Lumley, Charlotte Rampling, Donovan, Marianne Faithful, Diane Keaton, Steven Spielberg, Elton John, Uri Geller, Chris Tarrant, Dolly Parton, Liza Minnelli, Timothy Dalton, Al Green, Hayley Mills, Cher, Priscilla Presley, Barry Manilow, Sylvester Stallone, Cheech of Cheech and Chong, Tommy Lee Jones, Oliver Stone, Susan Sarandon, Neil Young, Bill Clinton, Malcolm McLaren and Ian Lavender (yes – even stupid boy Private Pike would now qualify as one of Dad's Army's old soldiers)

So there you are – not a curly white perm among them. Although Barry Manilow might suit one.

TIPS ON HOW TO APPEAR YOUNGER THAN YOU ACTUALLY ARE

Speak in monosyllables apart from the word 'whatever' which you should use constantly.

Tippex out the liver spots on the back of your hands.

Paint your neck so those skin-folds look like a trendy scarf.

Tell people your varicose veins are part of an elaborate detailed tattoo design.

If people phone you at 9 p.m. don't tell them they woke you up.

Learn to lip-read so you don't have to keep saying 'Eh?'

Don't leave your teeth on the mantelpiece.

Try liposuction using an attachment on your Dyson vacuum cleaner.

GIVEAWAYS THAT WILL TELL PEOPLE YOU ARE OVER 60

Turning the music down and the TV up

Having to ask for translations for phrases such as 'chill'

Being an expert on every medical condition out there

Reminiscing about when there was no swearing on TV

Your idea of a pin-up is Marlon Brando, Brigitte Bardot or perhaps Her Majesty Queen Elizabeth as an attractive young filly

Telling people there's nothing worth watching on television these days – and then doing nothing but watch TV all day

Videoing daytime quiz shows

A GUIDE TO HOW OTHERS WILL NOW PERCEIVE YOU

Someone who needs to be offered a seat on the bus

Someone who needs to be spoken to slowly and loudly

Someone who would appreciate a nice cardigan for Christmas

The originator of all odd smells

Only of interest to politicians at election time and family members who think they might be mentioned in your will

Someone who will still be crossing when the green man starts flashing

Elderly, infirm and of a nervous disposition

NAMES YOU CAN NOW EXPECT TO BE CALLED ON A REGULAR BASIS

Senior citizen

Old-timer

Coffin-dodger

Wrinkle-merchant

Victor (or Mrs) Meldrew

Countdown-watcher

Gramps or Granny

THE MAIN EVENTS IN YOUR LIFE YOU CAN NOW LOOK FORWARD TO

 Getting free prescriptions

 Watching your family growing up and making their way in the world – and at long last leaving you in peace!

 Your own stairlift

Reduced prices on just about everything
– except health insurance

 The fashion trends of your youth
becoming recognised as classics

 Only 15 years till you qualify for a winter
fuel allowance

 Never having to work again – no matter
how much you might want to

New hips – at long last you can be genuinely bionic!

THE MAIN EVENTS IN YOUR LIFE IT'S LESS EASY TO LOOK FORWARD TO

Getting breathless blowing out your birthday cake candles

Using your free prescriptions

 Watching your family growing up and making a pig's ear of their lives, and realising whatever you tried to teach them, they weren't listening

 Having your first chamber pot – for 'emergencies'

 Seeing the classic films of your youth remade and ruined

 Being given tickets for a Dave Dee, Dozy, Beaky, Mick & Tich revival tour

Having people talk about you as though
you're not actually there while popping
toffees in your mouth whether
you asked for them or not

CONVERSING WITH YOUNG PEOPLE (PART 1)

What you say and what they hear

'Isn't my new grandson/daughter lovely?' =
'I'm available for babysitting 24/7.'

'I can't see his father in him, can you?' = 'Who
is his father really?'

'You must come over for Sunday dinner soon.'
= 'I'll show you how to cook properly.'

'When I was young, we didn't have much but
we were happy.' = 'I was a saddo even then.'

'I was out at work by the time I was fourteen.'
= 'I was a Victorian child chimney sweep.'

'I'm not feeling too well.' = 'Congratulations!
You are about to come into your inheritance!'

STATISTICALLY SPEAKING

Now some worrying information. According to a recent survey the average cost of raising children is £7,889 per year or around £165,669 if you're stuck with them up to their twenty-first birthday.

But it doesn't stop there. There's also the costs of getting them through university or set up in a career. This is now estimated to be in the region of £25,572.

So if you've bestowed two of the little varmints on the world that's a grand total of £382,482.

Meanwhile the average cost of a home in Britain is now around the £200,000 mark.

So that's £582,482 you could have forked out just on having a family.

Take a good look at them. Be honest with yourself. Was it really worth it?

Well of course it was! Don't fret for a moment over the fact that the individuals shuffling miserably round your kitchen have cost you the equivalent of a really good win on *Who Wants To Be A Millionaire*.

Meanwhile, if you've drunk two pints of beer each and every day since you were 18, (and who could blame you with your family) that would represent a lifetime's consumption of 30,680 pints. Today the average price is £2.25 a pint. So your 30,680 pints has cost you around £69,030 in today's money.

If you smoke as well (and who could blame you with the stress of having to find all the money) that will also have cost you a mighty (cigarette) packet since you started puffing away over forty years ago. Back in the mid 60s a pack of twenty fags cost one old silver sixpence and the box didn't inform you in large black letters that its contents were out to kill you. Today the price is around £4.79. So let's call that an average price of £2.41 over the past forty years and that's another £73,865 you've slowly burnt your way through. In a way it's a blessing that smoking shortens your life a bit. Think of the money that will save you.

So all in all as a sixty-year-old, the combined cost of ruining your health with booze and fags and perhaps ruining your sanity by having a family could have amounted to £725,377.

Wouldn't it be terrible if the bill for all of this appeared in your letterbox tomorrow?

PEOPLE WHO ACHIEVED GREAT THINGS AFTER THE AGE OF 60

Winston Churchill was 65 when he became wartime leader.

John Wayne didn't get his first Oscar until the age of 62.

Louis Armstrong was 66 when he had his
first UK number one hit single
('What a Wonderful World').

Ronald Reagan didn't become President of the
USA until he was 69 – could be
some wait, Arnie!

NOW YOU'RE 60 THE FOLLOWING WILL BE YOUR NATURAL ENEMIES

Stairs

Food you have to chew

Small print

The TV and video tuning menus

People with *no* manners

Your own body

A LIST OF CONTROVERSIAL OPINIONS YOU WILL NOW BE EXPECTED TO HOLD

 Music went down the flusher when The Beatles started in my humble opinion.

 There are no gay animals in the wild.

 You should only have a ring through your nose if you're a pig.

 I don't care if they're black, white, brown or sky-blue pink, but...

My parents used to thrash me every day when I was a child and it never did me any harm...

 The only good reason not to reintroduce the ducking stool is because of the drought restrictions...

CONVERSING WITH YOUNG PEOPLE (PART 2)

What they say and what you hear

'How do you prune a rose bush?' = 'Can you come round and prune my rose bush?'

'Would you like to come over for dinner?' = 'There's a good takeaway nearby. Maybe you'd like to pay as well?'

'Could you come over and help me with my electrics?' = 'If you fry it doesn't matter quite so much.'

'I've got you a special birthday present this year.' = 'Have you got round to making your will yet?'

THINGS YOU CAN NOW GET AWAY WITH THAT YOU COULDN'T PREVIOUSLY

Saying exactly what you think

Making no effort whatsoever to lose weight

 Flirting outrageously with members of the opposite sex

 Cosmetic surgery

 Acting like the grumpy old git you know you've always been really

THINGS YOU SHOULD HAVE ACHIEVED BY NOW

 Being able to nod off during even the noisiest family gathering

 Knowing your alcohol limit

 Being able to set the video

 Being able to prepare an answerphone message without any jokes or silly voices

 Being an expert on every garden and house plant there is

THINGS YOU ARE NOW LIKELY TO HAVE IN YOUR HOME

 A fluffy toilet-seat cover

 A security spyhole in the front door

 A selection of nick-nacks on the mantelpiece

 Net curtains

 The complete published works of Catherine Cookson

 A packet of Werther's Original

A framed copy of every single school photo ever taken of your children and their children

 A mug dedicated to the best grandmother/father in the world (NB other people have been presented with this award as well)

THINGS THAT YOU WILL TAKE A SUDDEN INTEREST IN

Trimming bushes in your garden
into unusual shapes

Loyalty card points

Money-off coupons

The shocking prices of things these days

Whether your heart is still beating

CONVERSING WITH YOUNG PEOPLE (PART 3)

Words of wisdom you are now entitled to share with your juniors

'You feel exactly the same inside when you're 60 as you do when you're 20.'

'You're never too young to start a pension, you know.'

'Before you know it, you'll be as old as I am...'

'Don't let the buggers grind you down.'

'The way the world is now I'm glad
I'm not young.'

THINGS YOU'LL FEEL SMUG ABOUT

Having all your own hair

Having all your own teeth

Being able to tell youngsters you actually remember the 60s (even though you can't remember what happened yesterday)

Watching young people make the same mistakes you made and doing nothing to stop them

Having a no-claims bonus record that pre-dates the birth of the person you deal with at the insurance company

Having seen every single episode of
Coronation Street since it began

Going to a funeral and coming
home again afterwards

HOORAY! THINGS YOU'LL NEVER HAVE TO DO AGAIN

 Get your kids through university

 Give birth/attend a birth

 Feel like you need to resist temptation

 Do your bit for the environment – now you're 60 you can do what the hell you like and take the environment with you

BOO! THINGS YOU WON'T BE DOING AGAIN

Seeing in the New Year and enjoying it

Staying awake through an entire late-night film

 Setting the fashion world alight

 Having a one-night stand – one night would definitely be too long

 Moving any part of your body too quickly

 The lotus position

SHATTERING MOMENTS TO COME SOON

You bend down to see if you can still touch your toes and then forget what you went down there for

Someone offering to help you across the road

Taking more than one go to get up off the sofa

Learning the value of your childhood toys on
Antiques Roadshow

Your (or your partner's) semi-annual erection
becomes an annual semi-erection

THINGS YOU CAN EXPECT FOR YOUR BIRTHDAY

 Chocolates with soft centres

 Books in large print

 Vouchers – because 'old people are so difficult to buy for'

 A subscription to a nostalgia magazine

A gadget to help you find your keys

 An alarm in case you fall over in the garden – how old do these people think you are?

 Framed pictures of your grandchildren which you then have no choice but to put on permanent display

EXPRESSIONS THAT WILL DATE YOU

Courting (as in 'Are you courting yet dear?')

Making love (in the nothing-more-than-kissing-and-cuddling sense)

Wireless (meaning radio, not Internet access)

Gramophone

The flicks (the cinema)

Snaps (photographs)

71

Bread (money)

Daddyo

Hipster

Toodle pip

Ying tong iddle I po

Flippin' kids

See you later, alligator

GADGETS THAT ONLY THE OVER 60s WILL REMEMBER

Crystal set radios

'Box Brownie' cameras

TVs with just one channel

3D stereoscope viewers

Dolly tub and dolly peg (for washing your clothes with... and that's before we even get on to washboards)

Half-timbered cars (e.g. the Morris Minor Traveller)

X-ray specs (to enable you to see through your own hand!)

Toys you had to wind up rather than put batteries in

BEING 60 IS...

... being too old for work but too
young for retirement.

... a time when the only jogging you have to
do is with your memory.

... being too old for pot, too young for a
chamber pot

... when you have a lifetime of memories,
half of which you can't recall at
this particular moment.

... being too old for a walk on the wild side but
too young for a walk-in bath.

... when you find work a lot less fun and fun a
lot more work.

THINGS YOU SHOULD NOT HAVE IN YOUR HOME

 Any of your children for a start

 Clothes that you might fit into again one day – let's face it, you won't

 A budgie – people will think you're at least 80

 That old guitar you still only know three chords on

 A surveillance camera in the front window to gather evidence of misbehaviour by your neighbours

An unlicensed firearm

AARGHH! THINGS YOU NEVER THOUGHT WOULD HAPPEN

You forget your own birthday

You find korma curry a bit hot

Even your children are starting to look old

The sound of a dripping tap causes you to become desperate to go to the toilet

You start to enjoy hearing about other peoples' operations

You hear yourself say something to your children that your mother always used to say to you and which you always hated

You look for your glasses for half an hour and then find them on top of your head

YOUR NEW OUTLOOK ON LIFE

Your idea of multi-tasking is sleeping and not dribbling at the same time

Your idea of a white-knuckle ride is travelling on an escalator

Your idea of a dangerous sport is tiddlywinks

Your idea of being carried up to bed is your nightly trip on the stairlift

Your idea of a takeaway delivery boy is the
man from Meals on Wheels

You don't care where your spouse goes as
long as you don't have to go with them

You don't have to worry about additives any
more as you need all the preservatives
you can get

YOUR NEW WEEKLY HIGHLIGHTS

Trimming your ear and nasal hair

The local free paper being delivered

Buying your lottery ticket

**Reading the '25 years ago today'
section in the newspaper**

**Bumping into long-lost friends in the
doctor's waiting room**

THINGS YOU WILL DESPERATELY TRY TO AVOID

 Moving to a bungalow

 Fitting a handrail along the stairs

 Thermal socks

 Any item of clothing involving the word 'incontinence'

 Social events designed specifically for old people

THOSE WERE THE DAYS!
NOSTALGIA FOR THE
OVER 60s

When a Chinese meal was the
ultimate in exoticism

When a 'windows problem' meant
a jammed sash

When a people carrier was a
double-decker bus

When a PC caught burglars, not bugs

When a website was a corner of the ceiling
that hadn't been dusted

When daytime television meant eight hours
watching the picture of that girl playing
noughts and crosses with a toy clown

THINGS YOU SHOULD NOT
HAVE IN YOUR CAR

Silly stickers such as 'My other car's a write-off'

A speed-trap avoidance device – at your age!

Tartan seat covers – they may be cosy but
they'll age you by 15 years

A spare set of dentures in the
glove compartment

A starting handle – if you have one of
these you should really think about
getting a newer model

THINGS YOU WON'T BE DOING
ON HOLIDAY ANY MORE

Midnight skinny-dipping

Thinking of 'having a go' at paragliding

 Starting the day's drinking session straight after breakfast

 Founding the local nudist beach by unilateral action

 Throwing the TV out of the hotel window – even if you could manage to lift it, think of the bill you'll get and besides the Spanish version of *Countdown* is on in a few minutes

REASONS TO BE CHEERFUL

All those charities you gave to –
it's payback time!

You'll always be younger than Clint Eastwood
and Elizabeth Taylor.

So far, despite everything you've done to
yourself, you've survived – clearly you
must be indestructible.

Your secrets are safe with your friends because
now they can't remember them either.

You are now officially entitled to have a
wicked twinkle in your eye.

www.summersdale.com